REALLY EASY GUITAR

TAYLOR SWIFT

22 SONGS WITH CHORDS, LYRICS & BASIC TAB

Cover photo © Getty Images / Dave J. Hogan

ISBN 978-1-7051-1355-4

Visit Hal Leonard Online at
www.halleonard.com

T0019600

Contact us:
Hal Leonard
7777 West Bluemound Road
Milwaukee, WI 53213
Email: info@halleonard.com

In Europe, contact:
Hal Leonard Europe Limited
42 Wigmore Street
Marylebone, London, W1U 2RN
Email: info@halleonardeurope.com

In Australia, contact:
Hal Leonard Australia Pty. Ltd.
4 Lentara Court
Cheltenham, Victoria, 3192 Australia
Email: info@halleonard.com.au

Back to December

Words and Music by Taylor Swift

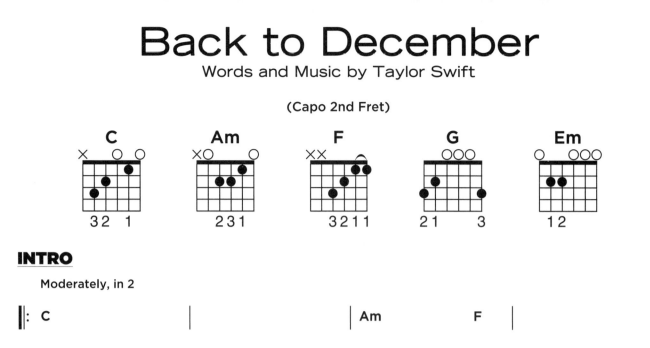

(Capo 2nd Fret)

INTRO

Moderately, in 2

‖: C | | Am F | :‖

VERSE 1

C   Am
I'm so glad you made time to see me.   How's life? Tell me how's you family?

F   C   G
I haven't seen them in a while.

C   Am
You've been good, busier than ever.   We small talk: work and the weather.

F   C   G
Your guard is up and I know why.

PRE-CHORUS 1

Am   G   C   F
Because the last time   you saw me it still burned in the back of your mind.

        Am   G   F
You gave me roses, and I left them there to die.

CHORUS

    C   Em
So, this is me swallowing my pride standing in front of you, saying I'm sorry for that night.

F   C   G
And I go { 1., 2. back to December all the time.
         { 3. back to December.

C   Em
It turns out freedom ain't nothing but missing you, wishing that I realized what I had when

F   C   G
you were mine. I go back to December, { 1., 3. turn   around and make it al -
                                      { 2. turn   around and change my own

F   Am   G
right. } I go back to December { 1., 2. all the time.
mind. }   { 3. turn around and change my

REPEAT INTRO

VERSE 2

```
     C                                      Am
       These days, I haven't been sleeping, staying up, playing back myself leaving,

     F                                      C      G
       When your birthday passed and I didn't call.

         C                                      Am
     Then I think about summer, all the beautiful times I watched you laughing from the passenger side and

     F                        C      G
       realized I loved you in the fall.
```

PRE-CHORUS 2

```
     Am                  G                C            F
       And then the cold came,   the dark days when fear crept into my mind.

                    Am            G      F
     You gave me all your love, and all I gave you was   goodbye.
```

REPEAT CHORUS

REPEAT INTRO

BRIDGE

```
             Am        F          C        G
     I miss your tan skin, your sweet smile, so good to me, so right:

                  Am          F                    C          G
     and how you held    me in your arms that September night,   the first time you ever saw me

     Am  N.C.                     F   N.C.
     cry.   Maybe this is wishful thinking,     probably mindless dreaming.

     C                          G      C  G
       If we loved again, I swear I'd love you right.

           Am        G              F
     I'd go back in time and change it, but I can't.

           Am          G      F
     So if the chain is on your door,   I under - stand.
```

REPEAT CHORUS

```
     F            Am          G
     own mind.    I go back to December all the time.
```

OUTRO

```
     C      Am  F        C      Am   F
                   All the time.
```

Blank Space

Words and Music by Taylor Swift, Max Martin and Shellback

(Capo 5th Fret)

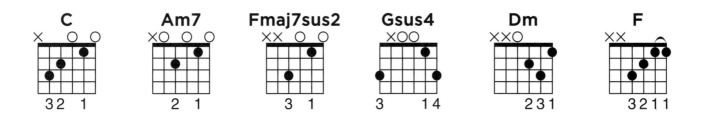

INTRO

Moderately slow

VERSE 1

C
Nice to meet you, where you been? I could show you incredible

Am7
things. Magic, madness, heaven, sins. Saw you there and I thought,

Fmaj7sus2
oh, my God, look at that face. You look like my next mistake.

Gsus4
Love's a game, wanna play?

C
New money, suit and tie, I can read you like a maga -

Am7
zine. Ain't it funny? Rumors fly, and I know you heard about

Fmaj7sus2
me. So, hey, let's be friends. I'm dying to see how this one ends.

Gsus4   **N.C.**
Grab your passport and my hand. *Spoken: I can make the bad guys good for a weekend.*

CHORUS

C
So it's gonna be forever or it's gonna go down in flames.

Am7
You can tell me when it's over, mm, if the high was worth the pain.

Dm
Got a long list of ex-lovers, they'll tell you I'm insane,

F
'cause you know I love the players and you love the game.

C
'Cause we're young and we're reckless, we'll take this way too far.

Am7
It'll leave you breathless, mm, or with a nasty scar.

Dm
Got a long list of ex-lovers; they'll tell you I'm insane.

F   **N.C.**
But I've got a blank space, baby,   and I'll write your name.

REPEAT INTRO

VERSE 2

C
Cherry lips, crystal skies, I could show you incredible

Am7
things. Stolen kisses, pretty lies. You're the king, baby, I'm your

Fmaj7sus2
queen. Find out what you want, be that girl for a month.

Gsus4
Wait, the worst is yet to come. Oh, no.

C
Screaming, crying, perfect storms. I can make all the tables

Am7
turn. Rose garden filled with thorns. Keep you second guessing like,

Fmaj7sus2
"Oh, my God, who is she?" I get drunk on jealousy.

Gsus4   **N.C.**
But you'll come back each time you leave. *'Cause darling, I'm a nightmare dressed like a daydream.*

REPEAT CHORUS

BRIDGE

N.C.
Boys only want love if it's torture. Don't say I didn't say I didn't warn you.

Boys only want love if it's torture. Don't say I didn't say I didn't warn you.

REPEAT CHORUS

Cardigan

Words and Music by Taylor Swift and Aaron Dessner

(Capo 1st Fret)

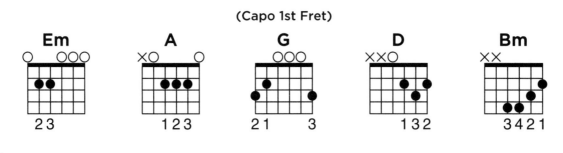

INTRO

Slow

N.C. ‖

VERSE 1

Em   A
  Vintage tee, brand new phone,   high heels on cobblestones.

G   A
  When you are young, they assume you know nothing.

VERSE 2

Em   A
  Sequin smile, black lipstick, sensual politics.

G   A
  When you are young, they assume you know nothing.

CHORUS 1

D   A
  But I knew you, dancing in your Levi's, drunk under a streetlight. I...

G   A
  I knew you, hand under my sweatshirt, baby, kiss it better. I...

Em   A
  And when I felt like I was and old cardigan under someone's bed,

G   A
  you put me on and said I was your fav'rite.

VERSE 3

Em   A
  A friend to all is a friend to none.   Chase two girls, lose the one.

G   A
  When you are young, they assume you know nothing.

CHORUS 2

```
      D                               A
      But I knew you, playing hide-and-seek and giving me your weekends. I...

      G                                   A
      I knew you, your heartbeat on the High Line once in twenty lifetimes. I...

      G                               Bm
      And when I felt like I was and old cardigan under someone's bed,

      D                               G                 Bm     A      G
      you put me on and said I was your fav'rite.
```

BRIDGE

```
              G                               Bm
      To kiss in cars    and downtown bars was all we need - ed.

              A                               G
      You drew stars around my scars, but now I'm bleeding.
```

CHORUS 3

```
      D                               A
      'Cause I knew you, stepping on the last train, marked me like a bloodstain. I...

      G                       A
      I knew you, tried to change the ending. Peter losing Wendy. I...

      D                       A
      I knew you, leaving like a father, running like water. I...

      G                                       A
      And when you are young, they assume you know nothing.
```

CHORUS 4

```
                      D                               A
      But I knew you'd lin - ger like a tatoo kiss. I knew you'd haunt    all of my "what ifs."

                  G                               A
      The smell of smoke    would hang around this long 'cause I knew ev - 'rything when I was young.

                  D                       A
      I knew I'd curse    you for the longest time, chasing shad - ows in the grocery line.

                  G                       A
      I knew you'd miss    me once the thrill expired and you'd be stand - ing in my front porch light.

                      Em                      A
      And I knew you'd come back    to me. You'd come back    to me,

                  G                       A
      and you'd come back    to me, and you'd come back.
```

OUTRO

```
      G                               Bm
      And when I felt like I was and old cardigan under someone's bed,

      D                       G
      you put me on and said I was your fav'rite.
```

Everything Has Changed

Words and Music by Taylor Swift and Ed Sheeran

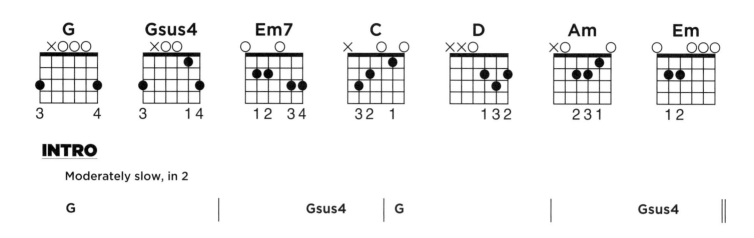

INTRO

Moderately slow, in 2

| G | | Gsus4 | G | | Gsus4 |

VERSE 1

G   Em7
All I knew this morning when I woke

C   D   N.C.
is I know something now, know something now I didn't before.

G   Em7
And all I've seen since eighteen hours ago

C   D
is green eyes and freckles and your smile in the back of my mind, making me feel right.

PRE-CHORUS 1

G   Am
I just wanna know you better, know you better, know you better now.

C   Em   D
I just wanna know you better, know you better, know you better now.

G   Am
I just wanna know you better, know you better, know you better now.

C   Em   D
I just wanna know you, know you, know you.

CHORUS 1

G   Em
'Cause all I know is we said hello and your eyes look like coming home.

D   C
All I know is a simple name. Everything has changed.

G   Em
All I know is you held the door. You'll be mine and I'll be yours.

D   C
All I know since yesterday is everything has changed.

REPEAT INTRO

VERSE 2

```
G                 Em7
And all my walls      stood tall, painted blue.

C                        D                    N.C.
But I'll take them down,    take them down and open the door for you.

G              Em7
And all I feel       in my stomach is butterflies,

C                                    D
the beautiful kind. Making up for lost time, taking flight, making me feel right.
```

REPEAT PRE-CHORUS 1

REPEAT CHORUS 1

BRIDGE

```
Em                    C              G              D
Come back and tell me why   I'm feeling like I missed   you all this time.

Em                    C              G              D
And meet me there tonight.   And let me know that it's   not all in my mind.
```

PRE-CHORUS 2

```
G                            Am
I just wanna know you better, know      you better, know you better now.

C                    Em    D
I just wanna know you, know      you, know you.
```

REPEAT CHORUS 1

CHORUS 2

```
G                    Em
All I know is we said hello.     So, dust off your highest hopes.

D                    C
All I know is pouring rain    and everything has changed.

G                        Em
All I know is a newfound grace. All my days I'll know your face.

D                    C  N.C.
All I know since yesterday        is everything has changed.
```

Exile

Words and Music by Taylor Swift, William Bowery and Justin Vernon

(Capo 6th Fret)

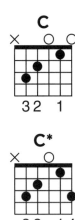
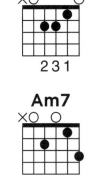
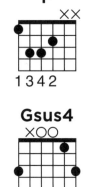
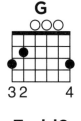

INTRO

Moderately slow

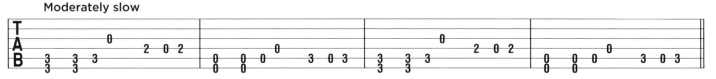

VERSE 1

C   Am
I can see you standing, honey,   with his arms around your body.

C   Am
Laughing but the joke's not funny at all.

C   Am
And it took you five whole minutes   to pack us up and leave me with it,

C   Am
holding all this love out here in the hall.

CHORUS 1

F   G   Am   G
I think I've seen this film before,   and I didn't like the ending.

F   G   Am   G
You're not my homeland anymore,   so what am I defending

F   G   Am   C
now? You were my town, now I'm in exile, seeing you out.

F   G   Am   *G
I think I've seen this film before.   *(So I'm leaving out the side door.)

*2nd time only

INTERLUDE

C   Am   C   Am
Ooh,   ooh,   ooh,

VERSE 2

   C   Am
I can see you staring, honey,   like he's just your understudy,

   C   Am
like you'd get your knuckles bloody for me.

   C   Am
Second, third and hundreth chances   balancing on breaking branches,

   C   Am
those eyes add insult to injury.

CHORUS 2

   F   G   Am   G
I think I've seen this film before,   and I didn't like the ending.

   F   G   Am   G
I'm not your problem anymore,   so who am I offending

   F   G   Am   C
now? You were my crown, now I'm in exile, seeing you out.

   F   G   Am   G
I think I've seen this film before,   so I'm leaving out the side door.

BRIDGE

   C*   Am7   Gsus4   Fadd9
So, step right out. There is no amount of crying I can do for you.
                                                    All   this

   C*   Am7
                                                    You
time, we always walked a very thin line. You didn't even hear me
 Gsus4   Fadd9   C*
didn't even hear me   out.   I   gave so man - y signs.
out.   You never gave a warning sign.   All   this   time, I never learned to read your
 Am7   Gsus4
Never learned to read my mind.   You never turned things a - round.   I
mind.   I couldn't turn things a - round   'cause you never gave a warning
 Fadd9   *C*   Am7   Gsus4   Fadd9
gave so many signs.} So many signs,   so many signs. {You didn't even see the signs.
sign. }
                    *To Outro 2nd time

REPEAT CHORUS 1

REPEAT BRIDGE

OUTRO

        C*   Am7
All this time   I never learned to read your mind,   I couldn't turn things a-
            so man -   y   times, so man -   y   signs.
 Gsus4   Fadd9
round. You never gave a warning   sign,   never gave a warning
                   You never gave a warning sign.
 C*   Am7   Gsus4   Fadd9
sign.   Ah,   ah.

I Knew You Were Trouble

Words and Music by Taylor Swift, Shellback and Max Martin

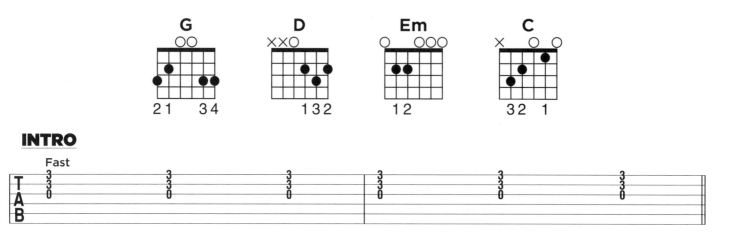

INTRO

Fast

VERSE 1

G   D
Once upon a time a few mistakes ago, I was in your sights, you got me alone.

      Em   C
You found me, you found me, you found me, ee, ee, ee, ee.

G   D
I guess you didn't care and I guess I liked that. And when I fell hard, you took a step back

      Em   C
without me, without me, without me, ee, ee, ee, ee.

PRE-CHORUS 1

  G   D
   And he's long   gone when he's next to

Em   C
me. And I realize   the blame is on me, 'cause

CHORUS

Em   C   D   G   D
I knew you were trouble when you walked in,   so shame on me now.

Em   C   D   G   D
   Flew me to places I've never been   till you put me down. Oh,

Em   C   D   G   D
I knew you were trouble when you walked in,   so shame on me now.

Em   C   D   *G   *D
   Flew me to places I've never been.   Now I'm lying on the cold, hard

                                      *Tacet 1st time

Em   C   D   G   D
ground. Oh   oh,   trouble, trouble, trouble.

Em   C   D   G   D
   Oh   oh,   trouble, trouble, trouble.

VERSE 2

G   D

No apologies, he'll never see you cry. Pretends he doesn't know that he's the reason why

      Em   C

you're drowning, you're drowning, you're drowning, ing, ing, ing , ing.

       G   D

And I heard you moved on from whispers on the street. A new notch in your belt is all I'll ever be.

      Em   C

And now I see, now I see, now I see, ee, ee, ee, ee.

PRE-CHORUS 2

  G   D

   He was long   gone when he met

Em   C

me. And I realize   the joke is on me. Hey!

REPEAT CHORUS

BRIDGE

           C   Em

And the saddest fear comes creeping in

           C   D

that you never loved me or her, or anyone, or anything. Yeah,

REPEAT CHORUS

OUTRO

Em   C   D   G   D

I knew you were trouble when you walked in.   Trouble, trouble, trouble.

Em   C   D   G   N.C.

I knew you were trouble when you walked in.   Trouble, trouble, trouble.

Look What You Made Me Do

Words and Music by Taylor Swift, Jack Antonoff, Richard Fairbrass,
Fred Fairbrass and Rob Manzoli

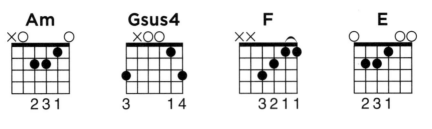

INTRO

Moderately fast

VERSE 1

Am

I don't like your little games, don't like your tilted

stage, the role you made me play of the fool, no, I don't like you.

I don't like your perfect crime, how you laugh when you

lie. You said the gun was mine. Isn't cool. No, I don't like you.

PRE-CHORUS

Am

But I got smarter, I got harder in the nick of time.

Gsus4

Honey, I rose up from the dead, I do it all the time.

F   **E**

I've got a list of names and yours is in red, underlined.   I check it once, then I check it twice. Oh!

CHORUS

Am

Ooh, look what you made me do, look what you made me

do, look what you just made me do, look what you just made me...

Ooh, look what you made me do, look what you made me

do, look what you just made me do, look what you just made me...

VERSE 2

Am
I don't like your kingdom keys, they, once belonged to

me. You asked me for a place to sleep, locked me out and threw a feast.

Rap: The world moves on another day, another drama, drama,

but not for me, not for me, all I think about is karma.

And then the world moves on, but one thing's for sure: maybe I got mine but you'll all get yours.

REPEAT PRE-CHORUS

REPEAT CHORUS

BRIDGE

Am   **F**   **E**
I don't trust nobody and nobody trusts me.   I'll be the actress staring in your bad dreams.

Am   **F**   **E**
I don't trust nobody and nobody trusts me.   I'll be the actress staring in your bad dreams.

Am   **F**   **E**
I don't trust nobody and nobody trusts me.   I'll be the actress staring in your bad dreams.

Am   **F**   **E**
I don't trust nobody and nobody trusts me.   I'll be the actress staring in your bad dreams.

INTERLUDE

Am   **Gsus4**   **F**
        Spoken: I'm sorry, the old Taylor can't come to the phone right now.   Why?

E   **N.C.**
 Oh,   'cause she's dead! Oh!

REPEAT CHORUS

OUTRO-CHORUS

Am
Ooh, look what you made me do, look what you made me

Gsus4
do, look what you just made me do, look what you just made me...

F
Ooh, look what you made me do, look what you made me

E   **N.C.**
do, look what you just made me do, look what you just made me do.

Love Story

Words and Music by Taylor Swift

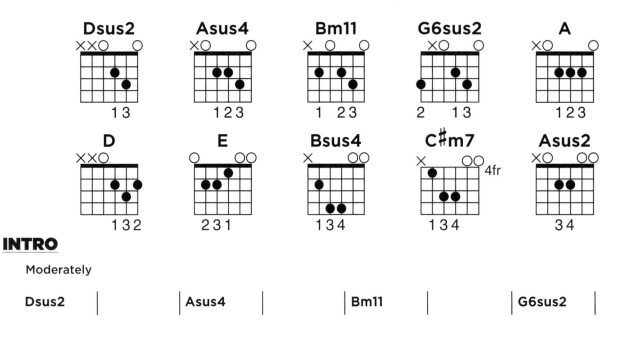

INTRO

Moderately

| Dsus2 | | | Asus4 | | | Bm11 | | | G6sus2 | | ‖

VERSE 1

Dsus2   G6sus2
We were both young when I first saw you. I close my eyes and the flashback starts.

           Bm11   G6sus2
I'm standing there   on a balcony in summer air.

VERSE 2

Dsus2   G6sus2
See the lights, see the party, the ball gowns. See you make your way through the crowd

           Bm11   Asus4   A
and say hello.   Little did I   know

           G6sus2   Asus4   Bm11   D
that you were Romeo. You were throwing pebbles, and my daddy said, "Stay away from Juliet."

           G6sus2   Asus4   Bm11 G6sus2   Asus4
And I was crying on the staircase, begging you, "Please don't go."   And I   said,

CHORUS 1

D   Asus4
"Romeo, take me somewhere we can be alone. I'll be waiting. All there's left to do is run.

Bm11   G6sus2   Asus4
You'll be the prince and I'll be the princess. It's a love story. Baby, just say yes."

INTERLUDE 1

| Dsus2 | | | | ‖

So,

VERSE 3

Dsus2   G6sus2
I sneak out to the garden to see you. We keep quiet 'cause we're dead if they knew.

             Bm11   Asus4   A
So, close your eyes, escape this town for a little while.

       G6sus2   Asus4   Bm11   D
'Cause you were Romeo, I was the scarlet letter, and my daddy said, "Stay away from Juliet."

       G6sus2   Asus4   Bm11 G6sus2   Asus4
But you were everything to me. I was begging you, "Please don't go."   And I   said,

REPEAT CHORUS 1

CHORUS 2

D   Asus4
"Romeo, save me. They're try'n' to tell me how to feel.   This love is difficult, but it's real.

Bm11   G6sus2   A
Don't be afraid. We'll make it out of this mess. It's a love story. Baby, just say yes."

INTERLUDE 2

D | |Asus4 | |Bm11 | |G6sus2 |A

BRIDGE

       Bm11 G6sus2   D   Asus4
I got tired of waiting,   wondering if you were ever coming around.

       Bm11   G6sus2   D   A
My faith in you was   fading   when I met you on the outskirts of town. And I said,

CHORUS 3

D   Asus4
"Romeo, save me. I've been feeling so alone. I keep waiting for you, but you never come.

     Bm11   G6sus2   Asus4   A N.C.
Is this in my head? I don't know what to think." He knealt to the ground and pulled out a ring and said,

CHORUS 4

E   Bsus4
"Marry me, Juliet, you never have to be alone. I love you and that's all I really know.

 C♯m7   Asus2   Bsus4
I talked to your dad. Go pick out a white dress. It's a love story. Baby, just say

OUTRO

E   Bsus4
  yes." Oh, oh, oh,   oh, oh, oh,

C♯m7   Asus2   E
  oh. 'Cause we were both young when I first saw you.

Mean

Words and Music by Taylor Swift

(Capo 4th Fret)

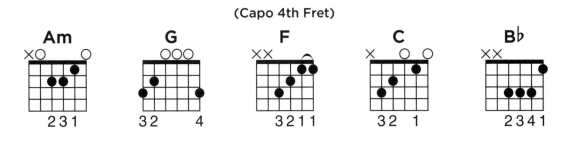

VERSE 1

Fast

Am   **G**   **F**
You, with your words like knives and swords and weapons that you use against me,

Am   **G**   **F**
you have knocked me off my feet again, got me feeling like a nothing.

Am   **G**   **F**
You, with your voice like nails on a chalkboard, calling me out when I'm wounded.

Am G   **F**
You,   picking on the weaker man.

PRE-CHORUS 1

G   **C**   **F**
Well, you can take me down   with just one single blow.

G   **F**   **N.C.**
But you   don't know what you don't know.

CHORUS

C   **G**   **Am**   **F**
{ Someday,} I'll be living in a big old city,
{ someday,}
  *(mean)
   **Bkgd. sung 4th time only.*

C   **G**   **F**
and all you're ever gonna be is mean. **(Yeah)
                         **3rd time only.

C   **G**   **Am**   **F**
Someday, I'll be big enough so you can't hit me,

C   **G**   **F**
and all you're ever gonna be is mean. Why you gotta be so

INTERLUDE 1

C | |**Bb**   **C** | ||
   mean?

VERSE 2

```
Am              G                       F
You, with your switching sides and your wildfire lies and your humiliation,

Am      G               F                       N.C.
you have pointed out my flaws again, as if I don't already see them.

Am               G                    F
   I walked with my   head down, trying to block you out 'cause I'll never impress you.

Am    G         F
I just  wanna feel okay again.
```

PRE-CHORUS 2

```
G                               C           F           G
   I'll bet you got pushed around,   somebody made you cold.   But the cycle ends right now,

          F                                           N.C.
'cause you can't lead me down that road and you don't know what you don't know.
```

REPEAT CHORUS

INTERLUDE 2

```
C         |         | B♭  C  |         | F    |    G  | F    |         ||
mean?                                                              And I can
```

BRIDGE

```
G                           C           F
see you years from now in a bar,   talking over a football game,

G                           C           F
   with that same big loud opinion but   nobody's listening.

G                       Am      G   F
   Washed up and ranting about the same old bitter things.

G                       Am   G    F
Drunk and grumbling on about how  I     can't sing. But all you are is
```

INTERLUDE 3

```
C    G    Am    F         C       G       Am        F
  mean.               All you are is mean, and a liar, and pathetic, and alone in life,

    C     G      Am      F
and mean, and mean, and mean, and mean. But
```

REPEAT CHORUS (2 TIMES)

```
C
  mean?
```

The 1

Words and Music by Taylor Swift and Aaron Dessner

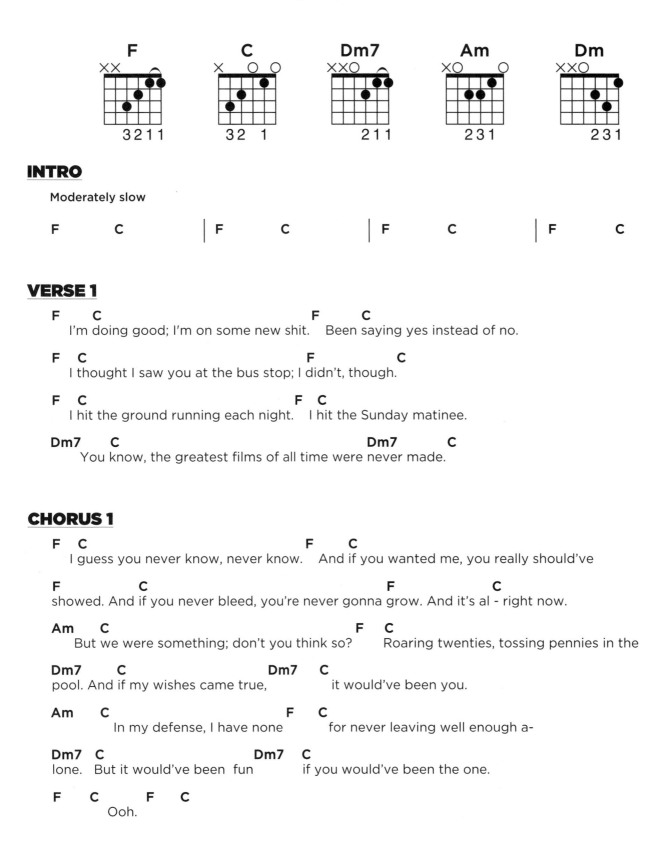

INTRO

Moderately slow

| F | C | | F | C | | F | C | | F | C |

VERSE 1

F   **C**   **F**   **C**
I'm doing good; I'm on some new shit.   Been saying yes instead of no.

F   **C**   **F**   **C**
I thought I saw you at the bus stop; I didn't, though.

F   **C**   **F**   **C**
I hit the ground running each night.   I hit the Sunday matinee.

Dm7   **C**   **Dm7**   **C**
You know, the greatest films of all time were never made.

CHORUS 1

F   **C**   **F**   **C**
I guess you never know, never know.   And if you wanted me, you really should've

F   **C**   **F**   **C**
showed. And if you never bleed, you're never gonna grow. And it's al - right now.

Am   **C**   **F**   **C**
But we were something; don't you think so?   Roaring twenties, tossing pennies in the

Dm7   **C**   **Dm7**   **C**
pool. And if my wishes came true,   it would've been you.

Am   **C**   **F**   **C**
In my defense, I have none   for never leaving well enough a-

Dm7 **C**   **Dm7**   **C**
lone. But it would've been fun   if you would've been the one.

F   **C**   **F**   **C**
Ooh.

VERSE 2

F   C   F   C
I had this dream: you're doing cool shit,   having adventures on your own.

F   C   Dm7   C
You'll meet some woman on the internet and take her home.

Dm   C   Dm   C
We never painted by the numbers, ba - by, but we were making it count.

Dm7   C   F   C
You know, the greatest loves of all time are over now.

CHORUS 2

F   C   F   C
I guess you never know, never know.   And it's another day waking up a-

Am   C   F   C
lone. But we were something; don't you think so?   Roaring twenties, tossing pennies in the

Dm7   C   Dm7   C
pool. And if my wishes came true,   it would have been you.

Am   C   F   C
In my defense, I have none   for never leaving well enough a-

Dm7 C   Dm7   C
lone.   But it would've been fun   if you would've been the one.

Am   C   F   C
I   persist and resist   the temptation to ask you:

 Dm7   C   Dm7   C
if one thing had been   different, would everything be   different today?

Am   C   F   C
We were something; don't you think so?   Rosé flowing with your chosen fami-

Dm7 C   Dm7   C
ly.   And it would've been sweet   if it could've been me.

Am   C   F   C
In my defense, I have none   for digging up the grave another

Dm7 C   Dm7   C
time. But it would've been fun   if you would've been the one.

Dm   C   Dm   C
Ooh.

Our Song

Words and Music by Taylor Swift

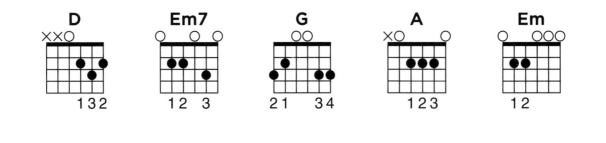

INTRO

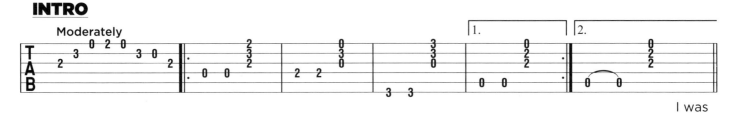

I was

VERSE 1

D   Em7   G   A
riding shotgun with my hair undone in the front seat of his car.

          D   Em7   G   A
He's got a one-hand feel on the   steering wheel, the other on my   heart.

D   Em7   G   A
 I look around, turn the radio down. He says, "Baby, is something wrong?"

D   Em7   G   A   N.C.
I say, "Nothing, I was just thinking how we don't have a song."   And he says,

CHORUS 1

D   Em7   G   A
 "Our song is a slamming screen door, sneaking out late, tapping on your window,

D   Em7   G   A
 when we're on the phone   and you talk real   slow 'cause it's late and your mama don't

D   Em7   G   A
know. Our song is the way you laugh, the first date. 'Man, I didn't kiss her and I should have.'

G   A   Em7   D   G   N.C.
 And when I got home, 'fore I said, "a-men," asking God   if He   could play it again."

INTERLUDE 1

D | Em7 | G | A

VERSE 2

D   Em7   G   A
I was walking up the front porch steps after   everything that   day

D   Em7   G   A
had gone all wrong, had been trampled on and lost and thrown a - way.

D   Em7   G   A
Got to the hallway, well on my way to my loving bed.

D   Em7   G   A
I almost didn't notice all the roses and the note that   said,

REPEAT CHORUS 1

INTERLUDE 2

1. | 2.

‖: D | Em7 | G | A   :‖ A | ‖
                                       Da, da, da, da.   I've

BRIDGE

Em   G
heard every album, listened to the radio,

D   A   Em7   G
waited for something to come along that was as good as our song.

CHORUS 2

D   Em7   G   A
'Cause our song is a slamming screen door, sneaking out late, tapping on his win-

D   Em7   G   A
dow, when we're on the phone   and he talks real slow 'cause it's late and his mama don't

D   Em7   G   A
know. Our song is the way he laughs, the first date, 'Man I didn't kiss him and I should have.'

G   A   Em7   D   G   A
And when I got home, 'fore I said, "a-men," asking God   if He   could play it again.

INTERLUDE 3

D Em7 G   A   D   Em7   G   A
                Play it again.   Oh, yeah

D Em7   G   A
    Oh, oh,   yeah.

OUTRO

D   Em7   G   A
I was riding shotgun with my hair undone in the front seat of his car.

D   Em7   G
I grabbed a pen and an old napkin and I   wrote down our song.

Picture to Burn

Words and Music by Taylor Swift and Liz Rose

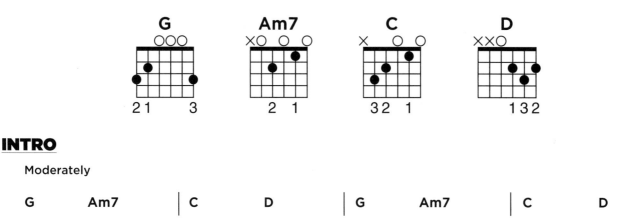

INTRO

Moderately

| G | Am7 | | C | D | | G | Am7 | | C | D | ‖ |

VERSE 1

G   Am7   C   D
State the obvious, I didn't get my perfect fantasy.

G   Am7   C   D
I realize   you love yourself   more than you could ever love me.

G   Am7   C   D
So, go and tell your friends   that I'm obsessive and

G   Am7   C   D   C
crazy. That's fine, you won't mind if I say, and by the way, I hate that

CHORUS 1

G   Am7   C   D
stupid old pickup truck you never let me drive.

        G   Am7   C   D
You're a redneck heartbreak who's really bad at lying.

G   Am7   C   D
So, watch me strike a match   on all my wasted time.

    C   D
As far as I'm concerned, you're just another picture to burn.

INTERLUDE 1

| G | Am7 | | C | D | | ‖ |

VERSE 2

```
G                 Am7              C         D
  There's no time      for tears, I'm just sitting here planning my revenge.

G                 Am7              C           D
  There's nothing stopping me, I'm going out with all    of your best friends.

G           Am7        C          D
  And if you come around    saying "sorry" to me,

    G             Am7          C          D
  my daddy's gonna show you how sorry you'll be. 'Cause I hate that
```

REPEAT CHORUS 1

INTERLUDE 2

```
G      Am7      | C       D      | G      Am7     | C      | D                ||
                                                                          And
```

BRIDGE

```
C                         D
  if you're missing me, you better keep it to yourself,

    C              G          D
  'cause coming back around here would be bad for your health.
```

CHORUS 2

```
            G        Am7         C          D
  'Cause I hate that stupid old pickup truck you never let me drive.

          G        Am7         C          D
  You're a redneck heartbreak who's really bad at lying.

G              Am7         C         D
  So, watch me strike a match    on all my wasted time.

  C                    D
In case you haven't heard, I really, really hate that
```

REPEAT CHORUS 1

OUTRO

```
G   Am7   C       D              G    Am7     C          D
      Burn, burn, burn, baby, burn.      You're just another picture to burn.

G   Am7   C     D          G
          Let it burn.
```

Safe & Sound
from THE HUNGER GAMES

Words and Music by Taylor Swift, T-Bone Burnett, John Paul White and Joy Williams

(Capo 7th Fret)

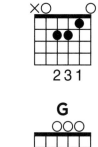

INTRO

Slow

VERSE 1

Dm   Am   F   C   C/B
I remember tears streaming down your face when I said I'll never let you go,

     Dm   Am   F   C
when all those shadows almost killed your light.

Dm   Am   F   C   C/B
I remember you said, "Don't leave me here alone."

   G   C   Fmaj7
But all that's dead and gone and past tonight.

CHORUS 1

Fmaj7   C   G
    Just close your eyes, the sun is going

Fmaj7   C   G
down. You'll be all right, no one can hurt you

Fmaj7   C   G   Am   G   F#m7♭5
now. Come morning light you and I'll be safe and sound.

REPEAT INTRO

VERSE 2

Dm   Am   F   C   C/B
Don't you dare look out your window, darlin', everything's on fire.

      Dm   Am   F   C
The war outside our door keeps raging on.

Dm   Am   F   C
Hold on to this lullaby

G   Fmaj7
even when the music's gone, gone.

REPEAT CHORUS 1

BRIDGE

Fmaj7   G   Am   G
Ooh.   Ooh,   oh, oh, oh.

Fmaj7   G   Am   G
Ooh.   Ooh,   oh, oh, oh, oh.

CHORUS 2

Fmaj7   C   G
    Just close your eyes.

Fmaj7   C   G
    You'll be all right.

Fmaj7   C   G   Am   G   F#m7♭5
    Come morning light you and I'll be safe and sound.

OUTRO

Play 3 times

‖: Fmaj7 | C   G | Fmaj7 | C   G   :‖
Ooh,   ooh.   Ooh,   ooh.

Shake It Off

Words and Music by Taylor Swift, Max Martin and Shellback

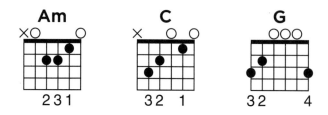

VERSE 1

Fast

          Am   **C**
I stay out too late,   got nothing in my brain;

                    G
that's what people say, mm, mm. That's what people say, mm, mm.

          Am   **C**
I go on too many dates,   but I can't make them stay; at least

                    G
that's what people say, mm, mm. That's what people say, mm, mm.

PRE-CHORUS 1

          Am   **C**
But I keep cruising; can't stop, won't stop moving.

                    G
It's like I got this music in my mind saying, "It's gonna be alright."

CHORUS

          Am   **C**
'Cause the players gonna play, play, play, play, play, and the haters gonna hate, hate, hate, hate, hate.

      G
Baby, I'm just gonna shake, shake, shake, shake, shake. I shake it off, I shake it off.

          Am   **C**
Heartbreakers gonna break, break, break, break, break, and the fakers gonna fake, fake, fake, fake, fake.

      G
Baby, I'm just gonna shake, shake, shake, shake, shake. I shake it off, I shake it off.

VERSE 2

              Am   **C**
I never miss a beat;   I'm lightning on my feet,

                        G
and that's what they don't see, mm, mm. That's what they don't see, mm, mm.

              Am   **C**
I'm dancing on my own;   I make the moves up as I go,

                        G
and that's what they don't know, mm, mm. That's what they don't know, mm, mm.

PRE-CHORUS 2

        Am   C
But I keep cruising; can't stop, won't stop grooving.

                    G
It's like I got this music in my mind saying, "It's gonna be alright."

REPEAT CHORUS

BRIDGE

  Am   C
I shake it off, I shake it off. I, I, I shake it off, I shake it off.

  G
I, I, I shake it off, I shake it off. I, I, I shake it off, I shake it off.

BREAKDOWN

N.C.
Spoken: "Hey, hey, hey! Just think: while you've been getting down and out about the liars and the dirty,

dirty cheats of the world, you could've been getting down to this sick beat!"

Rap: My ex man brought his new girlfriend. She's like, "Oh my God!" But I'm just gonna shake.

And to the fella over there with the hella good hair, won't you come on over, baby?

We can shake, shake, shake.   Yeah,   oh.

REPEAT CHORUS

OUTRO

  Am   C
I shake it off, I shake it off. I, I, I shake it off, I shake it off.

     G
I, I, I shake it off, I shake it off. I, I, I shake it off, I shake it off.

  Am   C
I shake it off, I shake it off. I, I, I shake it off, I shake it off.

     G
I, I, I shake it off, I shake it off. I, I, I shake it off, I shake it off.

  Am   C
I shake it off, I shake it off. I, I, I shake it off, I shake it off.

     G
I, I, I shake it off, I shake it off. I, I, I shake it off, I shake it off.

Teardrops on My Guitar

Words and Music by Taylor Swift and Liz Rose

(Capo 3rd Fret)

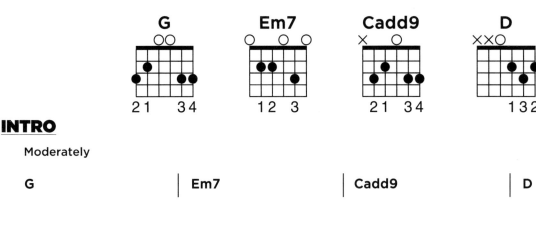

INTRO

Moderately

| G | | Em7 | | Cadd9 | | D | |

VERSE 1

G   Em7   Cadd9   D
Drew looks   at me,   I fake   a smile so he won't see

G   Em7   Cadd9   D
that I want   and I'm needing everything that we should be.

Em7   Cadd9
I'll bet she's beautiful,   that girl he talks about.

G   D
And she's got everything that I have to live without.

VERSE 2

G   Em7   Cadd9   D
Drew talks   to me,   I laugh   'cause it's just so funny

G   Em7   Cadd9   D
that I can't   even see   anyone when he's with me.

PRE-CHORUS 1

Em7   Cadd9
He says he's so in love,   he's finally got it right.

G   D
I wonder if he knows he's all I think about at night.

CHORUS 1

G   D
He's the reason for the teardrops on my guitar,

Em7   Cadd9
the only thing that keeps me wishing on a wishing star.

G   D   Em7   Cadd9
He's the song in the car   I keep singing. Don't know why   I do.

VERSE 3

```
G              Em7      Cadd9     D
Drew walks     by me,        can     he tell that I can't breathe?

G                    Em7           Cadd9            D
And there he goes,       so perfectly,        the kind of flawless I wish I could be.
```

PRE-CHORUS 2

```
Em7                          Cadd9
She better hold him tight,        give him all her love,

G                            D
look in those beautiful eyes    and know she's lucky 'cause
```

REPEAT CHORUS 1

INTERLUDE

```
‖: G                    | Em7            | Cadd9          | D              :‖
```

PRE-CHORUS 3

```
Em7                   Cadd9
So, I drive home alone.        As I turn out the light,

G                            D
I'll put his picture down and maybe get some sleep tonight.
```

CHORUS 2

```
G                            D
'Cause he's the reason for the teardrops on my guitar,

Em7                   Cadd9
the only one who's got enough of me to break my heart.

G                     D                          Em7      Cadd9
He's the song in the car   I keep singing. Don't know why      I do.

            G              D
He's the time     taken up, but there's never enough

            Em7                  Cadd9
and he's all       that I need to fall into.
```

OUTRO

```
G           Em7      Cadd9     D                   G
Drew looks     at me,      I fake   a smile so he won't see.
```

22

Words and Music by Taylor Swift, Shellback and Max Martin

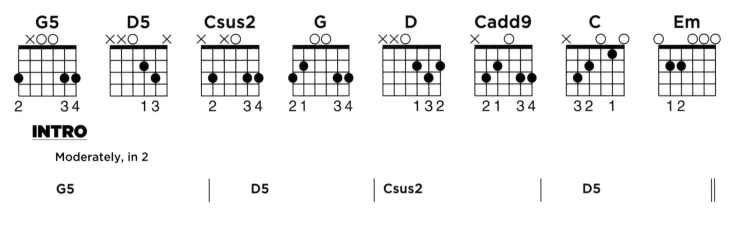

INTRO

Moderately, in 2

| G5 | | D5 | Csus2 | | D5 | |

VERSE 1

G5   D5   Csus2   D5
It feels like a perfect night   to dress up the hip - sters

G5   D5   Csus2   D5
and make fun of our ex - es.   Ah, ah. Ah, ah.

G5   D5   Csus2   D5
It feels like a perfect night   for breakfast at mid - night

G5   D5   Csus2   D5
to fall in love with stran - gers.   Ah, ah. Ah, ah.

PRE-CHORUS

G   D   Cadd9   D
Yeah,   we're happy, free, confused and lone - ly { 1. at the same / 2. in the best

G   D   Cadd9   D
time.} / way.} It's miserable and magical.   Oh,

G   D   Cadd9   D
yeah,   tonight's the night when we forget about the { 1. dead - / 2. heart -

G   D   Csus2
- lines.} / - breaks.} It's time.   Oh, oh.

CHORUS

G   D   C   Em
  I don't know about you,   but I'm feeling twenty two.

D   C   D
  Everything will be alright if   you keep me next to you.

G   D   C   Em
  You don't know about me,   but I'll bet you want   to.

D   C   D
  Everything will be alright if   we just keep dancing like we're

G   D   Cadd9   Em   D
twenty two,   twenty two.

VERSE 2

G5   D5   Csus2   D5
It seems like one of those nights. This place is too crowd - ed.

G5   D5   Csus2   D5
 Too many cool kids. Ah, ah. Ah, ah.

G5   D5   Csus2   D5
It seems like one of those nights, we ditch the whole scene

G5   D5 Csus2   D5
 and end up dream - ing   instead of sleep - ing

REPEAT PRE-CHORUS

REPEAT CHORUS

G   D   Cadd9   Em   D
 twenty two,   twenty two.

BRIDGE

G   D   Cadd9
It feels like one of those nights   we ditch the whole scene.

        Em   D
It feels like one of those nights we won't be sleeping.

G   D   Cadd9
It feels like one of those nights.   You look like bad news.

     Em   D
 I gotta have you. I gotta have you.

INTERLUDE

G D Cadd9   Em   D
  Oo,   oo,   yeah, ah, ah, ah, hey!

REPEAT CHORUS

G   D   Cadd9   Em   D
 twenty two,   twenty two.

REPEAT BRIDGE

We Are Never Ever Getting Back Together

Words and Music by Taylor Swift, Shellback and Max Martin

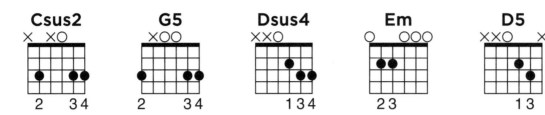

INTRO

Moderately, in 2

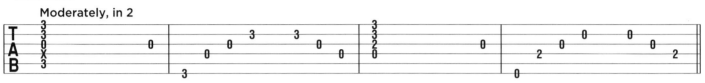

VERSE 1

Csus2   G5   Dsus4   Em

I remember when we broke up the first time, saying, "This is it. I've had enough."

          Csus2   G5   Dsus4   Em

'Cause like, we hadn't seen each other in a month when you said you needed space. * *Spoken: What?*

*Lyrics in italics are spoken throughout.

VERSE 2

Csus2   G5   Dsus4   Em

Then you come around again and say, "Baby, I miss you and I swear I'm gonna change, *trust me*."

Csus2   G5   Dsus4   Em

Remember how that lasted for a day? I say, "I hate you," we break up, you call me. *I love you.*

PRE-CHORUS

Csus2   G5   Dsus4   Em

Ooh,   { 1. we called it off again   last night.}
                   { 2. you called me up again   to-night.}

    Csus2   G5   Dsus4   Em

But ooh,   this time I'm telling you, I'm telling you

CHORUS 1

Csus2   G5   Dsus4   Em   D5

we   are never, ever, ever   getting back together.

Csus2   G5   Dsus4   Em   D5

We   are never, ever, ever   getting back together.

Csus2   G5   Dsus4   Em   D5

You go talk to your   friends, talk to my   friends, talk to me.

     Csus2   G5   Dsus4   N.C.

But we   are never, ever, ever,   ever   getting back to -

INTERLUDE 1

Csus2   **G5**   **Dsus4**   **Em**
gether.   Like,   ever.

VERSE 3

Csus2   **G5**   **Dsus4**   **Em**
I'm really gonna miss you picking fights. And me, falling for it, screaming that I'm right. And you would

Csus2   **G5**   **Dsus4**   **Em**
hide away and find your peace of mind with some *indie record that's much cooler than mine.*

REPEAT PRE-CHORUS

REPEAT CHORUS 1

INTERLUDE 2

Csus2   **G5**   **Dsus4**   **Em** **D5**   **Csus2**   **G5**   **Dsus4**   **Em** **D5**
gether. Ooh,   ooh.   Ooh,   oh, oh, oh.

BRIDGE

Csus2   **G5**   **Dsus4**   **Em**
I used to think   that we   were forever, ever.

Csus2   **G5** **Dsus4**   **Em**
And I used to say,   "Never say never."

Csus2   **G5**   **Dsus4**   **Em**
(Sigh) So he calls me up, and he's like, "I still love you." And I'm like,   I'm just,

Csus2   **G5**   **Dsus4** **N.C.**
I mean this is exhausting you know,   like, we are never getting back   together,   like ever. No,

REPEAT CHORUS 1

CHORUS 2

Csus2 **G5**   **Dsus4**   **Em** **D5**
we,   ooh,   getting back together.

Csus2 **G5**   **Dsus4**   **Em** **D5**
We,   ooh,   getting back together.

Csus2   **G5**   **Dsus4**   **Em** **D5**
You go talk to your   friends, talk to my   friends, talk to me.

Csus2 **G5**   **Dsus4**   **N.C.**
But we   are never, ever, ever,   ever,   getting back together.

White Horse

Words and Music by Taylor Swift and Liz Rose

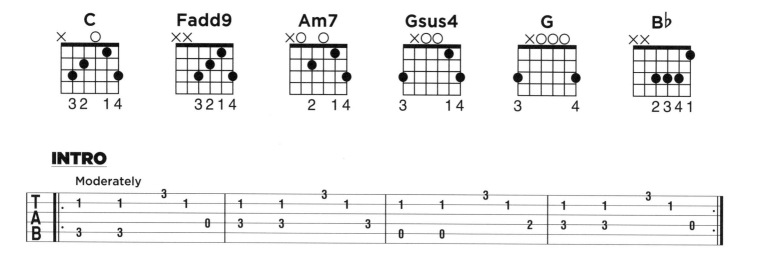

INTRO

Moderately

VERSE 1

C   Fadd9   Am7   Fadd9
Say you're sorry, that face   of an angel comes out   just when you need it to

C   Fadd9   Am7   Fadd9
as I paced back and forth   all this time 'cause I honestly believed in   you.

Am7   Fadd9
Hold - ing on, the days   drag on. Stupid girl,

Gsus4   G
I should've known, I should've known   that I'm not a prin-

CHORUS 1

C   Am7   Fadd9   Gsus4   G
cess, this ain't a fair - y tale. I'm not the one   you'll sweep off her feet, lead her up the stairwell.

C   Am7   Fadd9   Gsus4 G
This ain't Hollywood, this is a small   town. I was a dream - er before you went and let me down.

Am7   G   Fadd9
Now it's too late for you and your white   horse to come around.

INTERLUDE

C | ‖

VERSE 2

```
C                 Fadd9                        Am7                  Fadd9
Maybe I was naïve,       got lost in your eyes and never really had a chance.

C                      Fadd9                   Am7                  Fadd9
My mistake, I didn't know to be in love you had to fight to have the upper hand.

     Am7              Fadd9             Gsus4            G
I had so many dreams about you       and me; happy endings, now I know    that I 'm not a prin-
```

REPEAT CHORUS 1

GUITAR SOLO

```
C              |  Am7           |  Fadd9          |  Gsus4       G        ||
```

BRIDGE

```
Am7           G        Fadd9   C            G      Fadd9
And there you are on your     knees,    begging for forgiveness,       begging for me.

C          G          Fadd9           Bb
Just like I always wanted,        but I'm so sor - ry.   'Cause I'm not your prin -
```

CHORUS 2

```
C                Am7               Fadd9                         Gsus4       G
cess, this ain't a fair - y tale. I'm gonna find       someone someday who might actually treat me well.

     C                  Am7                Fadd9                 Gsus4   G
This is a big world, that was a small      town there in my rear       view mirror disappearing now.

       Am7          G           Fadd9
And it's too     late for you   and your white        horse,

       Am7          G           Fadd9
now it's too     late for you   and your white        horse to catch me
```

OUTRO

```
C     Fadd9    Am7     Fadd9
now.        Oh,                    try and catch me now,

C     Fadd9    Am7        Fadd9             C
oh.                It 's too late        to catch me now.
```

Wildest Dreams

Words and Music by Taylor Swift, Max Martin and Shellback

(Capo 1st Fret)

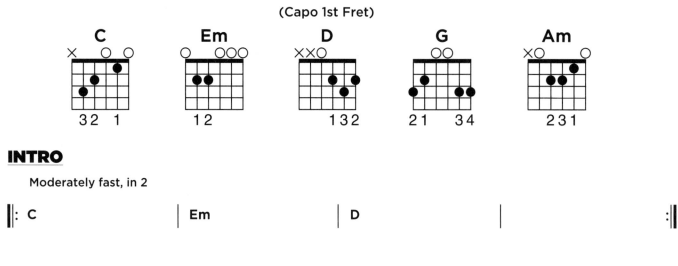

INTRO

Moderately fast, in 2

‖: C | Em | D | :‖

VERSE 1

           C   Em   D
He said, "Let's get out of this town, drive out of the city, away from the crowds."

             C   Em   D
I thought, "Heaven can't help me now.   Nothing lasts forever." But this is gonna take me down.

C   Em   D
   He's so tall and handsome as hell.   He's so bad but he does it so well.

C   Em   D
I can see the end as it begins. My one condition is:

CHORUS 1

G   D   Am   C
Say you'll remember me   standing in a nice dress, staring at the sunset, babe.

G   D   Am   C
Red lips and rosy cheeks.   Say you'll see me again even if it's just in your

G   D   Am   C
wildest dreams,   ah,   ha.

G   D   Am   C   *N.C.
Wildest dreams,   ah,   ha.

                         *1st time only

VERSE 2

         C   Em   D
I said, "No one has to know what we do." His hands are in my hair, his clothes are in my room,

         C   Em   D
and his voice is a familiar sound,   "Nothing lasts forever." But this is getting good now.

C   Em   D
   He's so tall and handsome as hell.   He's so bad but he does it so well.

C   Em   N.C.
And when we've had our very last kiss, my last request i - is.

BRIDGE

```
        G                    D                    Am        C
You'll see me in hindsight tangled up with you all night, burning it down.

G                            D                    Am        C
Someday when you leave me, I'll bet these memories follow you around.

         G                   D                    Am        C
You'll see me in hindsight tangled up with you all night, burning it down.

G                            D                    Am
Someday when you leave me, I'll bet these memories follow you around. (Follow you around.)
```

BREAKDOWN

```
G                    D            C
Say you'll remember me    standing in a nice dress, staring at the sunset, babe.

G                    D            C
Red lips and rosy cheeks.    Say you'll see me again even if it's just pretend.
```

CHORUS 2

```
G                    D            Am               C
Say you'll remember me    standing in a nice dress, staring at the sunset, babe.

G                    D                    Am        C
Red lips and rosy cheeks.    Say you'll see me again even if it's just in your

G          D     Am      C
wildest dreams,    ah,      ha.      In your

G          D     Am      C
wildest dreams,    ah,      ha.      In your

G          D     Am      C
wildest dreams,    ah,      ha.      In your

G          D     C
wildest dreams,    ah,      ha.
```

You Belong with Me

Words and Music by Taylor Swift and Liz Rose

(Capo 4th Fret)

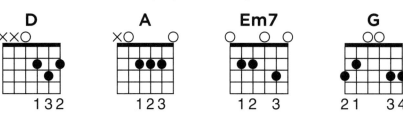

INTRO

Moderately fast

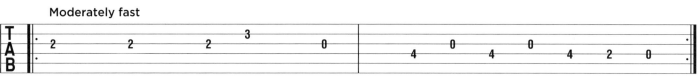

VERSE 1

D   A
You're on the phone with your girlfriend. She's upset. She's going off about something that you said.

Em7   G
'Cause she doesn't get your humor like I do.

D   A
I'm in the room, it's a typical Tuesday night. I'm listening to the kind of music she doesn't like.

Em7   G
And she'll never know your story like I do.

PRE-CHORUS 1

Em7   G   D   A
But she wears short skirts, I wear T-shirts, she's cheer captain and I'm on the bleachers,

Em7   G
dreaming 'bout the day when you wake up and find that what you're

A
looking for has been here the whole time. If you could

CHORUS 1

D   A
see that I'm the one who understands you. Been here all along. So why can't you

Em7   G   D
see you belong with me? You belong with me.

VERSE 2

D   A
Walking the streets with you in your worn out jeans, I can't help thinking this is how it ought to be.

Em7   G
  Laughing on a park bench, thinking to myself, "Hey, isn't this easy?"

     D
And you've got a smile that could light up this whole town.

  A
  I haven't seen it in a while since she brought you down.

Em7   G
  You say you're fine. I know you better than that. Hey, what you doing with a girl like that?

PRE-CHORUS 2

Em7   G   D   A
She wears high heels, I wear sneakers, she's cheer captain and I'm on the bleachers,

Em7   G
dreaming 'bout the day when you wake up and find that what you're

  A
  looking for has been here the whole time. If you could

CHORUS 2

D   A
see that I'm the one who understands you. Been here all along. So why can't you

Em7   G   D
see you belong with me? Standing by and waiting at your back door.

A   Em7   G
All this time how could you not know baby, you belong with me? You belong with me.

INTERLUDE

D | | A | | Em7 | | G |

BRIDGE

      Em7   G
Oh, I remember you driving to my house in the middle of the night.

    D   A
I'm the one who makes you laugh when you know you're 'bout to cry.

  Em7   G
I know your favorite songs and you tell me 'bout you dreams.

    D   A
Think I know where you belong. Think I know it's with me. Can't you

REPEAT CHORUS 2

OUTRO

D   A   Em7   G   D
  You belong with me. Have you ever thought just maybe you belong with me? You belong with me.

You Need to Calm Down

Words and Music by Taylor Swift and Joel Little

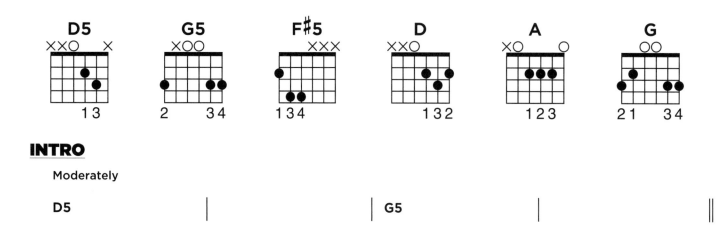

INTRO

Moderately

D5 | | G5 | ||

VERSE 1

D5
You are somebody that I don't know, but you're taking shots at me like it's Patrón, and I'm just like,

G5   **F♯5**
"Damn!   It's seven a.m.!"

D5
Say it in the street, that's a knockout; but you say it in a tweet, that's a copout. And I'm just like,

G5   **F♯5**
"Hey,   are you okay?"

           D5
And I ain't trying to mess with you self expression but I've learned the les-

son that stressing and obsessing 'bout somebody else is no

G5   **N.C.**   **F♯5**
fun.   And snakes and stones never broke my bones. So

CHORUS

D   **A**
oh, oh. (Oh, oh, oh, oh, oh, oh, oh, oh, oh!) You need to calm

G
down. You're being too loud. And I'm just like,

D   **A**
oh, oh. (Oh, oh, oh, oh, oh, oh, oh, oh, oh!) You need to just

G
stop. Like, can you just not step on { 1. my / 2. his } gown? You need to calm

INTERLUDE

D5
down.

VERSE 2

D5
You are somebody that we don't know, but you're coming at my friends like a missle. Why are you

G5
mad when you could be glad?

D5
Sunshine on the street at the parade, but you would rather be in the dark ages. Making that

G5   **F♯5**
sign   must have taken all night.

D5
You just need to take several seats and then try to restore the peace

and control your urges to scream about all the people you

G5   **N.C.**   **F♯5**
hate;   'cause shade never made anybody less gay. So

REPEAT CHORUS

BRIDGE

D5
down. And we see you over there on the internet, comparing other girls who are killing it;

G5
but we figured you out. We all know now we all got crowns. You need to calm

OUTRO-CHORUS

D
Oh,   oh. (Oh, oh, oh, oh, oh, oh, oh, oh, oh!) You need to calm
down.

G
down. You're being too loud. And I'm just like,

D   **A**
oh, oh. (Oh, oh, oh, oh, oh, oh, oh, oh, oh!) You need to just

G   **D**
stop. Like, can you just not step on our gowns? You need to calm down.

Fifteen

Words and Music by Taylor Swift

G	Cadd9	Em7	D	Em	C
○○	×　○	○　　○	××○	○　○○○	×　○　○
2 1　3 4	2 1　3 4	1 2　3 4	1 3 2	2 3	3 2　1

INTRO

Moderately

| G | Cadd9 | Em7 | Cadd9 ‖

VERSE 1

G   Cadd9
 You take a deep breath and you walk   through the doors.

     Em7   Cadd9
It's the morning of your very first day.

     G   Cadd9
You say, "Hi" to your friends you ain't seen in a while, try and stay

Em7   Cadd9
out of everybody's way.

G   Cadd9
 It's your freshman year and you're gonna be here for the next

Em7   Cadd9
 four years in this   town.

        G   Cadd9
Hoping one of those senior boys will wink at you and say,

     Em7   Cadd9
"You know, I haven't seen you around   before." 'Cause when you're

CHORUS 1

G   Em7   D   Cadd9
 fifteen and somebody tells you they love you, you're gonna believe them. And when you're

G   D   Em7   Cadd9
 fifteen feel - ing like there's noth - ing to figure out,   but,

Em   D   G   D Cadd9 D
 count to ten, take it in. This is life before you know who you're gon - na be.   Fifteen.

REPEAT INTRO

VERSE 2

G   Cadd9   Em7   Cadd9
You sit in class next to a red - head named Abigail and soon enough we're best friends,

G   Cadd9   Em7   Cadd9
Laughing at the other girls who think they're so cool. We'll be out of here as soon as we can.

   G   Cadd9   Em7   Cadd9
And then you're on your very first date and he's got a car and you're feeling like fly - ing.

     G   Cadd9
And your mama's waiting up and you're thinking he's the one

     Em7   Cadd9
and you're dancing 'round your room when the night ends, when the night ends. 'Cause when you're

CHORUS 2

G Em7   D   Cadd9
fifteen and somebody tells you they love you, you're gonna believe them. And when you're

G   D   Em7   Cadd9 Em
fifteen and your first kiss makes your head spin around, but, in your life you'll do things

D   G   D   Cadd9   D
greater than dating the boy on the foot - ball team. I didn't know it at fifteen.

INTERLUDE

G | Cadd9 | Em7 | Cadd9   D ||

BRIDGE

C   Em   D
When all you want - ed was to be want - ed, wish you could go back

   G   D   Cadd9   D
and tell yourself what you know now.

VERSE 3

G   Cadd9   Em7   Cadd9
Back then I swore I was gonna marry him someday, but I realized some bigger dreams of mine.

   G   Cadd9   Em7
And Abigail gave everything she had to a boy who changed his mind.

Cadd9
And we both cried. 'Cause when you're

CHORUS 3

G   Em7   D   Cadd9
fifteen and   somebody tells you they love   you, you're gonna believe   them. And when you're

G   D   Em7   Cadd9
fifteen, don't   forget to look   before you fall.

Em   D   G   D   Cadd9
I've found time can heal most   anything and you just might find who you're supposed to be.

Em   D   Cadd9   D
I didn't know who I was s'posed to be   at fifteen.

OUTRO

G   Cadd9   Em7   Cadd9
            La, la, la, la, la, la,   la, la, la, la.

G   Cadd9   Em7   Cadd9
La, la, la, la, la, la,   la, la, la, la.   La, la, la, la, la, la,   your very first

G   Cadd9   Em7   Cadd9
day.   Take a deep breath, girl.   Take a deep breath as you walk   through the doors.

GUITAR NOTATION LEGEND

Chord Diagrams

CHORD DIAGRAMS graphically represent the guitar fretboard to show correct chord fingerings.

- The letter above the diagram tells the name of the chord.
- The top, bold horizontal line represents the nut of the guitar. Each thin horizontal line represents a fret. Each vertical line represents a string; the low E string is on the far left and the high E string is on the far right.
- A dot shows where to put your fret-hand finger and the number at the bottom of the diagram tells which finger to use.
- The "O" above the string means play it open, while an "X" means don't play the string.

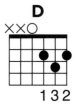

Tablature

TABLATURE graphically represents the guitar fingerboard. Each horizontal line represents a string, and each number represents a fret.

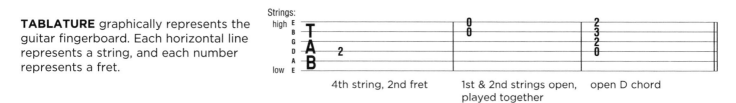

4th string, 2nd fret 1st & 2nd strings open, played together open D chord

Definitions for Special Guitar Notation

HAMMER-ON: Strike the first (lower) note with one finger, then sound the higher note (on the same string) with another finger by fretting it without picking.

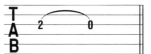

PULL-OFF: Place both fingers on the notes to be sounded. Strike the first note and without picking, pull the finger off to sound the second (lower) note.

LEGATO SLIDE: Strike the first note and then slide the same fret-hand finger up or down to the second note. The second note is not struck.

SHIFT SLIDE: Same as legato slide, except the second note is struck.

Additional Musical Definitions

N.C. • No chord. Instrument is silent.

 • Repeat measures between signs.

REALLY EASY GUITAR

Easy-to-follow charts to get you playing right away are presented in these collections of arrangements in chords, lyrics and basic tab for all guitarists.

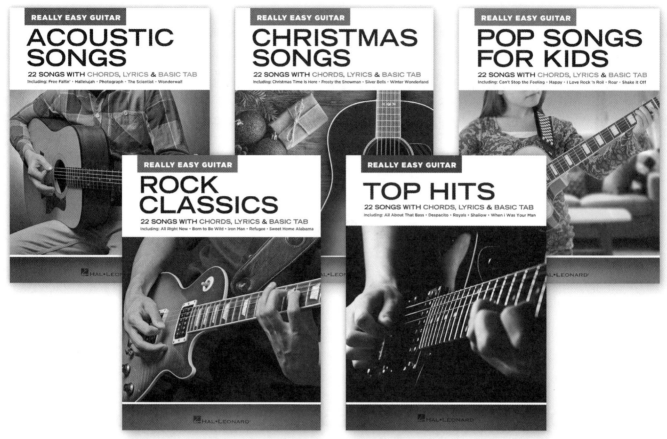

ACOUSTIC CLASSICS
22 songs: Angie • Best of My Love • Dust in the Wind • Fire and Rain • A Horse with No Name • Layla • More Than a Feeling • Night Moves • Patience • Time in a Bottle • Wanted Dead or Alive • and more.
00300600 ....$9.99

ACOUSTIC SONGS
22 songs: Free Fallin' • Good Riddance (Time of Your Life) • Hallelujah • I'm Yours • Losing My Religion • Mr. Jones • Photograph • Riptide • The Scientist • Wonderwall • and more.
00286663 ....$9.99

THE BEATLES FOR KIDS
14 songs: All You Need Is Love • Blackbird • Good Day Sunshine • Here Comes the Sun • I Want to Hold Your Hand • Let It Be • With a Little Help from My Friends • Yellow Submarine • and more.
00346031 ....$9.99

CHRISTMAS CLASSICS
22 Christmas carols: Away in a Manger • Deck the Hall • It Came upon the Midnight Clear • Jingle Bells • Silent Night • The Twelve Days of Christmas • We Wish You a Merry Christmas • and more.
00348327 ....$9.99

CHRISTMAS SONGS
22 holiday favorites: Blue Christmas • Christmas Time Is Here • Frosty the Snowman • Have Yourself a Merry Little Christmas • Mary, Did You Know? • Silver Bells • Winter Wonderland • and more.
00294775 ....$9.99

THE DOORS
22 songs: Break on Through to the Other Side • Hello, I Love You (Won't You Tell Me Your Name?) • L.A. Woman • Light My Fire • Love Her Madly • People Are Strange • Riders on the Storm • Touch Me • and more.
00345890 ....$9.99

BILLIE EILISH
14 songs: All the Good Girls Go to Hell • Bad Guy • Everything I Wanted • Idontwannabeyouanymore • No Time to Die • Ocean Eyes • Six Feet Under • Wish You Were Gay • and more.
00346351 ....$9.99

POP SONGS FOR KIDS
22 songs: Brave • Can't Stop the Feeling • Happy • I Love Rock 'N Roll • Let It Go • Roar • Shake It Off • We Got the Beat • and more.
00286698 ....$9.99

ROCK CLASSICS
22 songs: All Right Now • Born to Be Wild • Don't Fear the Reaper • Hey Joe • Iron Man • Old Time Rock & Roll • Refugee • Sweet Home Alabama • You Shook Me All Night Long • and more.
00286699 ....$9.99

TOP HITS
22 hits: All About That Bass • All of Me • Despacito • Love Yourself • Royals • Say Something • Shallow • Someone like You • This Is Me • A Thousand Years • When I Was Your Man • and more.
00300599 ....$9.99

halleonard.com